OUR LIVING WORLD

Humans

By **Jenny Tesar**

With Illustrations by Pedro Julio González

Series Editor: Vincent Marteka
Introduction by John Behler, *New York Zoological Society*

A BLACKBIRCH PRESS BOOK
WOODBRIDGE, CONNECTICUT

Published by Blackbirch Press, Inc.
One Bradley Road, Suite 205
Woodbridge, CT 06525

©1994 Blackbirch Press, Inc.
First Edition

Printed in Canada

10 9 8 7 6 5 4 3 2 1

Editorial Director: Bruce Glassman
Editor: Tanya Lee Stone
Assistant Editor: Elizabeth M. Taylor
Design Director: Sonja Kalter
Production: Sandra Burr, Rudy Raccio, Madeline Parker

Library of Congress Cataloging-in-Publication Data

Tesar, Jenny E.
   Humans / by Jenny Tesar; with illustrations by Pedro Julio González.—
1st ed.
        p.   cm. — (Our living world)
   Includes bibliographical references and index.
   ISBN 1-56711-048-7
   1. Human physiology—Juvenile literature. [1. Body, Human.] I. Title.
II. Series.
QP37.T45   1994
612—dc20
                                                                        93-44543
                                                                              CIP
                                                                               AC

Contents

***Introduction: What Does It Mean to Be "Alive"?
by John Behler   4***

1 ***Humans: The Overview   7***
Humans Are Mammals, 8 • Unique Characteristics of Humans, 10
The Earliest Humans, 15

2 ***The Senses: How Humans React   19***
How Humans See, 20 • How Humans Hear, 22 • The Sense of Balance,
24 • Sense Organs in the Skin, 25 • Maintaining a Proper Temperature,
26 • The Sense of Smell, 29 • The Sense of Taste, 29

3 ***Metabolism: How Humans Function   31***
Eating and Digesting Food, 32 • Getting Oxygen, 34 • Removing Wastes,
35 • Circulating Food, Oxygen, and Other Materials, 36

4 ***Reproduction and Growth   39***
The Reproductive System, 40 • Development of a Baby, 43 • From Birth
to Adulthood, 47

5 ***Fitting into the Web of Life   51***
Competing for Food, 52 • Changing the Environment, 54 • Saving
the Environment, 57

The Animal Kingdom   58
Glossary   60
For Further Reading   61
Index   62

What Does It Mean to Be "Alive"?

Introduction by John Behler,
New York Zoological Society

One summer morning, as I was walking through a beautiful field, I was inspired to think about what it really means to be "alive." Part of the answer, I came to realize, was right in front of my eyes.

The meadow was ablaze with color, packed with wildflowers at the height of their blooming season. A multitude of insects, warmed by the sun's early-morning rays, began to stir. Painted turtles sunned themselves on an old mossy log in a nearby pond. A pair of wood ducks whistled a call as they flew overhead, resting near a shagbark hickory on the other side of the pond.

As I wandered through this unspoiled habitat, I paused at a patch of milkweed to look for monarch-butterfly caterpillars, which depend on the milkweed's leaves for food. Indeed, the caterpillars were there, munching away. Soon these larvae would spin their cocoons, emerge as beautiful orange-and-black butterflies, and begin a fantastic 1,500-mile (2,400-kilometer) migration to wintering grounds in Mexico. It took biologists nearly one hundred years to unravel the life history of these butterflies. Watching them in the milkweed patch made me wonder how much more there is to know about these insects and all the other living organisms in just that one meadow.

The patterns of the natural world have often been likened to a spider's web, and for good reason. All life on Earth is interconnected in an elegant yet surprisingly simple design, and each living thing is an essential part of that design. To understand biology and the functions of living things, biologists have spent a lot of time looking at the differences among organisms. But in order to understand the very nature of living things, we must first understand what they have in common.

The butterfly larvae and the milkweed—and all animals and plants, for that matter—are made up of the same basic elements. These elements are obtained, used, and eliminated by every living thing in a series of chemical activities called metabolism.

Every molecule of every living tissue must contain carbon. During photosynthesis, green plants take in carbon dioxide from the atmosphere. Within their chlorophyll-filled leaves, in the presence of sunlight, the carbon dioxide is combined with water to form sugar—nature's most basic food. Animals need carbon, too. To grow and function, animals must eat plants or other animals that have fed on plants in order to obtain carbon. When plants and animals die, bacteria and fungi help to break down their tissues. This allows the carbon in plants and animals to be recycled. Indeed, the carbon in your body—and everyone else's body—may once have been inside a dinosaur, a giant redwood, or a monarch butterfly!

All life also needs nitrogen. Nitrogen is an essential component of protoplasm, the complex of chemicals that makes up living cells. Animals acquire nitrogen in the same manner as they acquire carbon dioxide: by eating plants or other animals that have eaten plants. Plants, however, must rely on nitrogen-fixing bacteria in the soil to absorb nitrogen from the atmosphere and convert it into proteins. These proteins are then absorbed from the soil by plant roots.

Living things start life as a single cell. The process by which cells grow and reproduce to become a specific organism— whether the organism is an oak tree or a whale—is controlled by two basic substances called deoxyribonucleic acid (DNA) and ribonucleic acid (RNA). These two chemicals are the building blocks of genes that determine how an organism looks, grows, and functions. Each organism has a unique pattern of DNA and RNA in its genes. This pattern determines all the characteristics of a living thing. Each species passes its unique pattern from generation to generation. Over many billions of years, a process involving genetic mutation and natural selection has allowed species to adapt to a constantly changing environment by evolving—changing genetic patterns. The living creatures we know today are the results of these adaptations.

Reproduction and growth are important to every species, since these are the processes by which new members of a species are created. If a species cannot reproduce and adapt, or if it cannot reproduce fast enough to replace those members that die, it will become extinct (no longer exist).

In recent years, biologists have learned a great deal about how living things function. But there is still much to learn about nature. With high-technology equipment and new information, exciting discoveries are being made every day. New insights and theories quickly make many biology textbooks obsolete. One thing, however, will forever remain certain: As living things, we share an amazing number of characteristics with other forms of life. As animals, our survival depends upon the food and functions provided by other animals and plants. As humans—who can understand the similarities and interdependence among living things—we cannot help but feel connected to the natural world, and we cannot forget our responsibility to protect it. It is only through looking at, and understanding, the rest of the natural world that we can truly appreciate what it means to be "alive."

Humans: The Overview

 More than 5 billion humans live on Earth. They live in every kind of environment—from the icy Arctic to hot tropical rainforests, from seashores to mountaintops, from tents in deserts to apartments in crowded cities.

Each of these humans is unique—different from every other person. Some people are tall, others are short. Some have dark skin, others have pale skin. Some have blue eyes, others have brown eyes.

Humans speak different languages, enjoy different games, work at different jobs, and practice different religions. But the differences among humans are very slight when compared with the ways in which they are all alike.

Humans also have many things in common with other living things. A human looks and acts very different from a pine tree. But both the human and

Opposite:
Humans are the most intelligent and the most powerful organisms on Earth. Although there are some ways in which the human species is unique, we still share many of our traits with all other living things.

the tree need food and air to survive. They both can react to changes in their surroundings. And they are both able to grow and reproduce.

Humans Are Mammals

Humans belong to a group of animals called mammals. Horses, tigers, monkeys, dogs, and kangaroos are other examples of mammals. Mammals get their name from the Latin word *mamma,* which means "breast." All female mammals have two or more mammary glands that produce milk. Females feed their young with this milk.

All mammals are vertebrates—they are animals with backbones. A backbone is made up of bones called vertebrae. At the top of the backbone is the skull. A backbone, skull, and other bones give the body its shape. They protect the stomach, heart, brain, and other soft organs. Together with the muscles, bones make movement possible.

Humans belong to a group of animals called mammals, which breast-feed their young with milk produced by mammary glands. Other mammals include cats, elephants, whales, and sheep.

It's Great to Be a Primate

Humans are members of a group of mammals known as primates. Apes, monkeys, and lemurs also are primates. These animals are the closest living relatives of humans.

The arms and hands of primates are different from those of all other animals. The lower part of each arm, called the forearm, has two long bones. These bones are arranged so that the arm can turn at the elbow.

Each hand has five fingers. The first finger is an opposable thumb. That is, the thumb can move toward the other fingers. This makes it possible for primates to hold objects in their hands.

Primates also have the most highly developed brains of all animals. And the best-developed brain of all belongs to humans.

Ape

Monkey

Lemur

Human

Mammals are endothermic, or warm-blooded. Their body temperature stays more or less the same, even though the temperature of their environment changes. Being warm-blooded makes it possible for these animals to live in cold places where most other animals could not survive.

Mammals are the only animals that have true hair, or fur. The hair insulates the body, helping to keep it warm. Because humans do not have as much hair as many other mammals, they must wear clothing to keep warm in cold weather. Hair, however, is very useful to humans. For example, hairs of the nose and ears keep out dust, as do eyelashes.

Mammals have the most highly developed brains of all animals. This makes mammals more intelligent than other animals. They can learn from experience and adapt very quickly to changes in their environment. The most intelligent of all the mammals are humans.

Unique Characteristics of Humans

Think of all the things humans can do that no other living things can do. We can build cars and bake cookies. We can write letters and play baseball. We can sail boats and invent computers. Activities such as these are possible because of characteristics that make humans different from all other living things. These unique characteristics involve the human brain, intelligence, language, posture, and hands.

The human brain Humans are not the biggest, strongest, or fastest animals. They don't even have the largest brains—that distinction belongs to the elephant. But humans are the smartest of all animals because they have the most complex and highly developed brains.

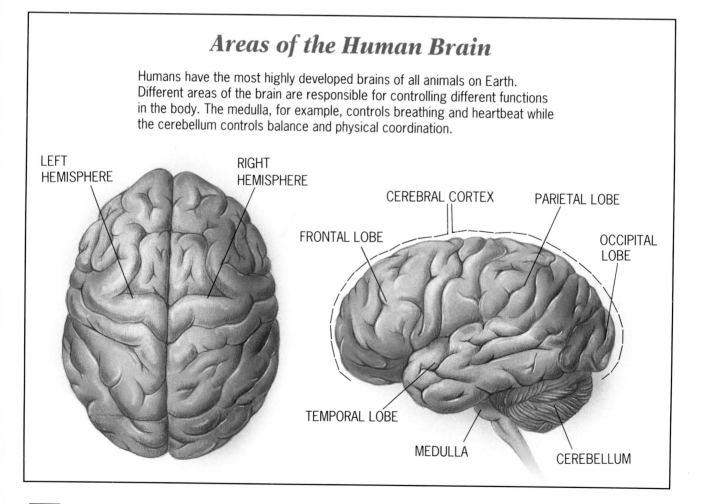

Areas of the Human Brain

Humans have the most highly developed brains of all animals on Earth. Different areas of the brain are responsible for controlling different functions in the body. The medulla, for example, controls breathing and heartbeat while the cerebellum controls balance and physical coordination.

LEFT HEMISPHERE

RIGHT HEMISPHERE

CEREBRAL CORTEX

PARIETAL LOBE

FRONTAL LOBE

OCCIPITAL LOBE

TEMPORAL LOBE

MEDULLA

CEREBELLUM

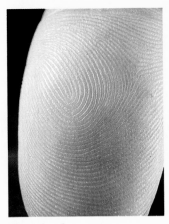
The brain of an adult human weighs about 3 pounds (1.5 kilograms). It is made up of billions of nerve cells, which connect to other nerve cells in the spinal cord, located inside the backbone. All these nerve cells connect with still more nerve cells throughout the entire body. Nerve cells carry messages to or from the brain. The messages are in the form of electrical signals—somewhat like the electrical signals that race through computers or over telephone lines. Some signals travel along the nerves at more than 200 miles (320 kilometers) per hour!

The brain has several main parts. Each performs certain tasks. The medulla, which is directly above the spinal cord, controls functions such as breathing and heartbeat. The cerebellum controls balance and body movements. The hypothalamus, in the center of the brain, regulates activities such as body temperature, thirst, and appetite.

The largest part of the human brain is the cerebrum, which makes up about 80 percent of the brain's weight. The cerebrum is divided into two major sections: the left hemisphere and the right hemisphere. Certain functions and abilities are controlled by either the left side or right side of the brain. Each hemisphere is divided into four areas, called lobes. The outer part of the cerebrum, the cerebral

cortex, is twisted and folded into grooves and ridges. This gives the cortex a very large surface area. No other animals have brains with such a large cortex.

Human intelligence A vast network of nerve cells are squeezed into the cerebral cortex. Different sections of the cortex are responsible for different activities. One section controls the movement of muscles in your arms and legs. Some sections handle information from the eyes, nose, and other sense organs. But the sections that help make humans unique are those for thinking, memory, and judgment.

The human brain enables humans to learn complex ideas, to communicate with verbal and written language, and to wonder and dream.

The cerebrum is the center of human intelligence. It is the part of the brain where learning takes place, ideas are imagined, problems are solved, and decisions are made. It is the part of the brain a person uses to remember what happened last Tuesday, decide which muscles to use, compose a song, invent a game, or enjoy a daydream.

Human language The ability to speak and write complex languages has given humans a great advantage over other organisms. Language makes it possible to share information and ideas. It lets humans benefit from one another's past experiences, including the experiences of humans who lived long ago.

Try to imagine what your world would be like without language. Imagine how difficult life would be if you didn't have parents and teachers who explained how to do things, if there were no books or television from which to learn, if the world's doctors and researchers had never been taught about diseases, operations, and medicines.

Human posture Humans are the only animals that can stand upright for long periods of time. They use only their two back limbs, or legs, for walking and running. Being able to stand upright means that arms and hands can constantly be used for other activities.

That's Intelligent, Man

Every kind of living thing is given a scientific name. This name is the same all over the world. The scientific name for humans is *Homo sapiens*. The name comes from Latin words meaning "intelligent man."

The Upstanding Human

The ability to stand upright gave humans a great advantage as they evolved. Whereas many other animals, such as gorillas, use their front limbs to walk or run, humans use only their legs. This ability has left human hands free to accomplish other tasks, including carrying objects and making and using tools.

Members of the Human Family

DRYOPITHICUS

First appeared about
12 million years ago

Ancient primate widely
thought to be direct
ancestor of living
African apes.

RAMAPITHICUS

About 14 million years
ago

Thought by many to
be the first hominid,
but its classification
is disputed—some
scientists believe it
was still a member
of the ape family.

AUSTRALOPITHICUS

More than 4 million
years ago

Very early member of
the human family.
Walked upright and
had a larger brain than
average ape species.
Often classified in
between an ape and
the first human
species, *Homo habilis.*

An upright posture also lets humans make better
use of their sharp eyes. It increases the area that they
can view and makes it much easier for them to see
straight ahead.

Human hands No other animal has hands as
flexible or as capable of such a wide variety of tasks.
Each human hand has a big, muscular thumb that
sticks out at an angle from the other fingers. The
thumb can be moved to touch the palm of the hand
and the tips of the other fingers. This makes it
possible to pick up and hold many kinds of objects,

HOMO HABILIS	HOMO ERECTUS	NEANDERTHAL HUMAN	CRO-MAGNON HUMAN	MODERN HUMAN
About 1.9 million years ago	About 1.6 million years ago	More than 100,000 years ago	100,000 years ago	About 40,000 years ago
Less robust jaw than australopithicus, smaller teeth, and a larger brain. Used primitive stone tools.	Limbs and skeleton much thicker than that of modern humans but very similar in bodily structure and proportion.	Shorter than modern human, longer skull, lower forehead, but a comparable brain size.	Shorter and broader face than Neanderthal, reduced brow ridge, and reduced incisor and canine teeth.	High brow, large brain cavity, lightest skeletal frame.

from a little bread crumb to a large puppy. It also makes it possible to carry books and rake leaves.

The Earliest Humans

Humans have lived on Earth for nearly 2 million years. This isn't very long when compared with other kinds of living things. Sponges and jellyfish have existed for more than 600 million years. Fish first appeared about 450 million years ago. Ferns developed about 300 million years ago. Horses appeared more than 50 million years ago.

No Bones About It

Ancient Neanderthal remains

In 1856, a group of workers found some bones in a cave in the Neander Valley near Dusseldorf, Germany. Scientists studied the bones and realized that they were from the skeleton of a person who lived tens of thousands of years ago. They named the person Neanderthal man.

Since then, many more remains of Neanderthals have been found in Europe and in parts of Asia and North Africa. Scientists have determined that Neanderthals existed from about 125,000 to about 40,000 years ago. They were shorter and had thicker bodies than modern humans. They had small, sloping foreheads and almost no chins. But their brains were comparable to those of humans today.

Knives, scrapers, and other stone tools have been found among Neanderthal fossils. Neanderthals hunted many kinds of animals, including extinct species such as mammoths, cave bears, and woolly rhinoceroses. They ate the animals' flesh and used their skins for clothing and shelter.

A Man on Ice, That's Nice

In 1991, two mountain climbers in the European Alps found the body of a man. The body had been hidden in thick layers of ice, but the ice had melted.

The body was very well preserved. People thought it had been trapped in the ice 40 or 50 years. But when scientists began to study the body, they discovered that it was 5,000 years old!

The ice had preserved the man's body, his axe, his deerskin clothing, and even tiny organisms inside his stomach. These remains tell us about life long ago and how the human body has changed in the past 5,000 years.

The kinds of humans that lived long ago no longer exist. They died out, or became extinct. We know these people existed because they left clues to how they looked and how they lived. These ancient clues are called fossils. Fossils are remains or traces of organisms that lived in the past. Most fossils are found in rocks.

Scientists have found bones, teeth, and footprints of early humans. Near these fossils, they have found remains of the plants and animals these people used as food. Scientists have also found ancient tools and the remains of fires, buildings, and clothing.

The very first humans looked quite different from modern humans. They were short, with small brains and ape-like faces. But they stood upright, had human-like teeth, and made simple tools of stone. Very slowly, over thousands of years, these humans changed. Eventually, they began to look more like modern humans. This gradual change in organisms is called evolution. Humans, like all living things, are still evolving. Humans who live 100,000 years from now will most probably look quite different from the humans of today.

These bones of ancient robust australopithecus were found in South Africa in 1936. Heavily built and vegetarian, australopithecines first appeared more than 4 million years ago.

The Senses: How Humans React

Imagine making a list of everything you know at this minute about your surroundings. Would the list be very long? It sure would! It would have to include descriptions of everything you see, every sound you hear, every odor you smell. It would have to include the feel of your clothing, the temperature of the air, and lots of other information.

Everything you know about the world comes to you through your eyes, ears, nose, and other sense organs. These structures gather an incredible amount of information. They see animals, smell roses, taste chocolate-chip cookies, feel warm breezes, and hear airplanes. Sense organs make it possible for you to enjoy your surroundings. They also protect you by warning of dangers in the surroundings.

Humans have some of the best-developed sense organs of all living things. These organs are always working, even while a person is sleeping.

Opposite:
Before you experience anything, it has to be detected by your senses. Seeing, smelling, touching, hearing, and tasting are all ways in which you get information about the world around you.

Color Conscious

Most mammals see the world in shades of black, gray, and white. Their eyes do not contain cone cells. Because humans have cone cells, they can distinguish more than 10 million shades of color!

Some humans are color-blind and cannot distinguish certain colors. In the most common form of color-blindness, red and green appear gray, blue, or yellow.

Information gathered by sense organs is sent along nerves to the brain. The brain then sends messages to muscles, telling them to respond to changes in the environment. For example, when your eyes see a mosquito on your leg, the eyes send a message to the brain. The brain sends a message to muscles in your arm and hand. Without thinking, you slap the mosquito. The process is extremely fast. It takes only a fraction of a second to respond to the information gathered by the eyes.

Special parts of the brain receive information from the sense organs. One area is responsible for sight, another area for hearing, and still other areas for smell, taste, touch, and so on.

How Humans See

Human eyes are very similar to the eyes of other mammals. They are shaped rather like balloons, and they are filled with clear fluids. Near the front of each eye is a transparent lens. Light passes through the lens and is focused on the back inside layer of the eye.

The human eye is similar in structure and function to the eyes of many other animals. Unlike most animals, however, the human eye can see color and can relay a three-dimensional image to the brain.

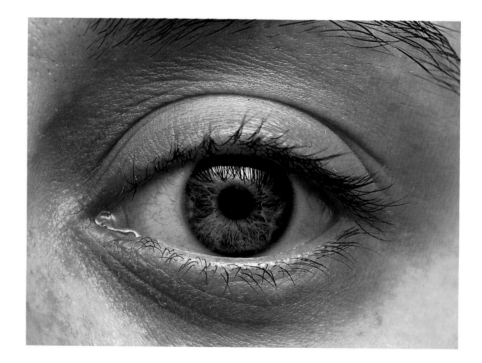

The Senses: How Humans React

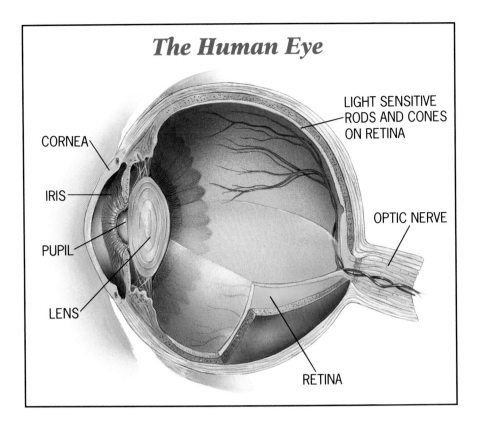

The Human Eye

CORNEA

IRIS

PUPIL

LENS

LIGHT SENSITIVE
RODS AND CONES
ON RETINA

OPTIC NERVE

RETINA

This layer, called the retina, contains light-sensitive cells called rods and cones. A human eye has about 135 million rods and cones. Light that strikes the rods and cones is changed into nerve impulses. These impulses travel along the optic nerve to the brain.

Cones are sensitive to color. They work best in bright light. Rods are sensitive only to black and white. They work well in dim light. Rods make it possible to see at night, when there is very little light.

Like monkeys and owls, humans have eyes that are located in the front of the head. This allows both eyes to see an object at the same time, which is called binocular vision. Because the eyes are a small distance apart, they see at slightly different angles. When the brain combines the two images, a three-dimensional image is formed. Animals with eyes on the sides of their heads, such as horses and robins, do not see in three dimensions. This makes it harder for them to judge distances and depths.

21

The Senses: How Humans React

How Humans Hear

When a person speaks, a dog barks, or a bell rings, sound waves form. These waves travel through air, water, and other materials. To be heard, they must be detected by sense organs called ears. A human has two ears, one on each side of the head.

The human ear has three parts: the outer ear, the middle ear, and the inner ear. The outer ear is the fleshy part outside the head. It directs sound waves through a canal toward the eardrum, which separates the outer ear from the middle ear. When the sound waves hit the eardrum, it vibrates. As the eardrum

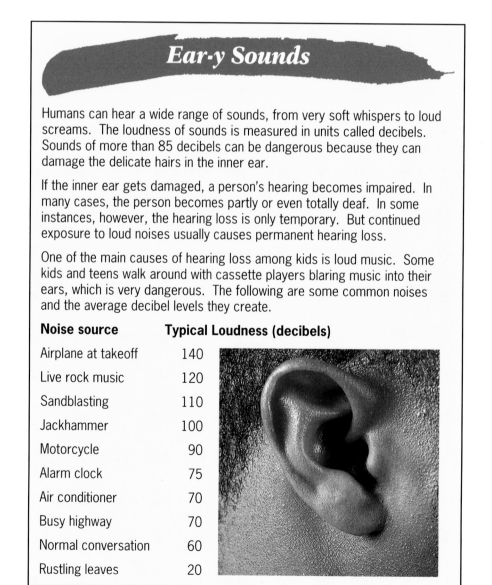

Ear-y Sounds

Humans can hear a wide range of sounds, from very soft whispers to loud screams. The loudness of sounds is measured in units called decibels. Sounds of more than 85 decibels can be dangerous because they can damage the delicate hairs in the inner ear.

If the inner ear gets damaged, a person's hearing becomes impaired. In many cases, the person becomes partly or even totally deaf. In some instances, however, the hearing loss is only temporary. But continued exposure to loud noises usually causes permanent hearing loss.

One of the main causes of hearing loss among kids is loud music. Some kids and teens walk around with cassette players blaring music into their ears, which is very dangerous. The following are some common noises and the average decibel levels they create.

Noise source	Typical Loudness (decibels)
Airplane at takeoff	140
Live rock music	120
Sandblasting	110
Jackhammer	100
Motorcycle	90
Alarm clock	75
Air conditioner	70
Busy highway	70
Normal conversation	60
Rustling leaves	20

The Senses: How Humans React

The Human Ear

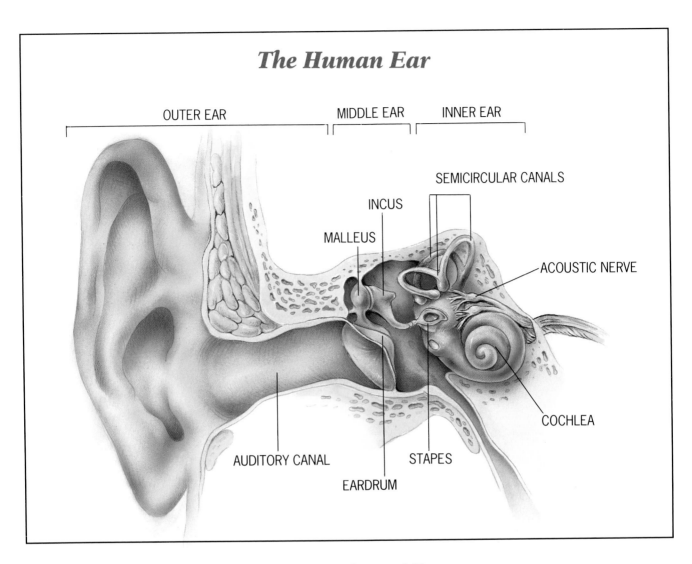

OUTER EAR   MIDDLE EAR   INNER EAR

SEMICIRCULAR CANALS

INCUS

MALLEUS

ACOUSTIC NERVE

COCHLEA

AUDITORY CANAL   STAPES

EARDRUM

vibrates, it causes three little bones in the middle ear to vibrate. These bones—the malleus, the incus, and the stapes—pass on the vibrations to the inner ear.

The main part of the inner ear, called the cochlea, is shaped like a snail shell. It is filled with fluid and contains thousands of tiny hairs. Each of the hairs is attached to a nerve ending. Sound vibrations cause the hairs to move. The movement is detected by the nerves, which carry the information to the brain.

Humans can hear many different sounds. But there are some sounds humans cannot hear that certain other animals can. For example, a "silent" dog whistle makes a very high sound that dogs can hear, but humans cannot.

23

The Sense of Balance

Ears are the organs that make it possible for humans and other mammals to hear. But ears also play an important role in maintaining a mammal's balance. The sense of balance lets a person tell "up" from "down," even when the eyes are closed. It lets the brain know if the body is standing up or lying down. Then the brain can tell muscles to act accordingly.

The inner ear has three structures called semicircular canals, filled with fluid (see diagram on page 23). When a person's head changes position, the fluid moves. This movement is detected by sense cells in the canals, which alert the brain. The brain then makes adjustments throughout the body in order to maintain balance.

Three structures in the inner ear, called semicircular canals, give humans their sense of balance. Sense cells detect the movement of fluid in the canals and send balance messages to the brain.

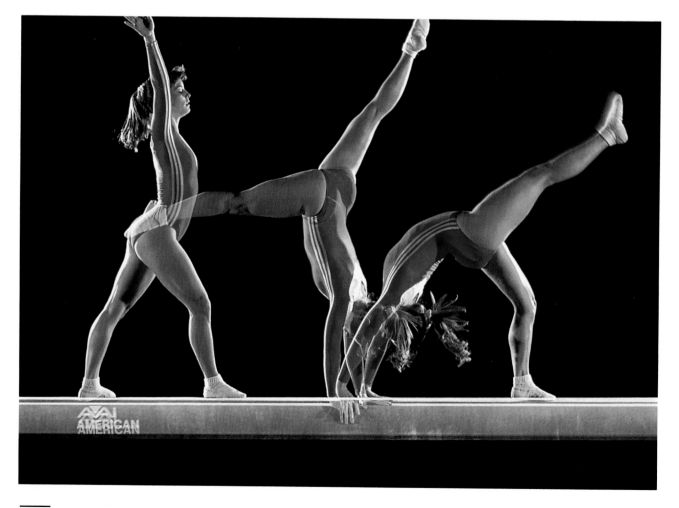

The Senses: How Humans React

Have you ever felt dizzy? Perhaps you were on a boat or on an amusement park ride. The constant movement caused the fluid in the semicircular canals to splash about. This sent lots of different messages to the brain, making you feel dizzy and maybe even seasick.

Other sense organs also help maintain balance. Signals from the eyes and from pressure organs on the bottoms of the feet are very important for this function.

Sense Organs in the Skin

Human skin has three major layers: the epidermis, which is the outside layer; the dermis, which is the middle layer; and the hypodermis, which is deepest inside. Several kinds of sense cells are located in the skin. These cells tell the brain about touch, pressure, pain, heat, and cold. For example, touch cells help you identify many kinds of objects even when your eyes are closed. Pain cells on the surface of your eyes detect bits of dirt. Heat cells tell the brain that your body has touched a hot stove.

These sense organs are not evenly distributed over the body. Structures like the fingertips are densely packed with cells that are very sensitive to touch. Other parts, like the skin on the back of the hand, have fewer touch cells and are therefore less sensitive to touch. But there are more pain cells on the back of the hand than on the fingertips.

The small hairs that cover a person's body also are important in the sense of touch. When something touches a hair, it bends. This bending is detected by a nerve ending at the base of the hair. These nerves make it possible for a person to be aware of even the smallest touch, such as a tiny insect walking over hairs on the arm.

25

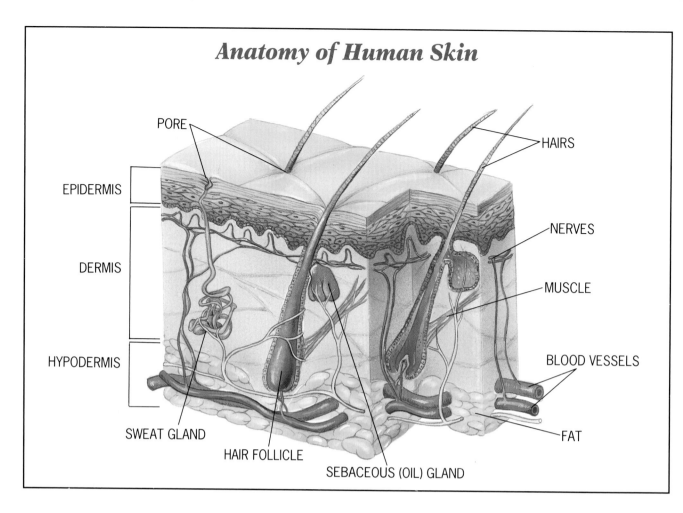

Anatomy of Human Skin

PORE

HAIRS

EPIDERMIS

NERVES

DERMIS

MUSCLE

HYPODERMIS

BLOOD VESSELS

SWEAT GLAND

FAT

HAIR FOLLICLE

SEBACEOUS (OIL) GLAND

Maintaining a Proper Temperature

Humans and other warm-blooded animals have to maintain a body temperature that is nearly the same all the time. Special sense cells gather information about the environment's temperature. These cells send the information to the part of the brain that controls body temperature. The brain lets us know when we should put on or take off jackets and other clothes we use to feel comfortable.

A person going outdoors on a cold day may shiver if he or she is not wearing enough clothing. Shivering is the body's way of keeping warm. Messages from the brain close the tiny holes, or pores, in the skin. This prevents body heat from escaping through the pores. Other messages from the brain tell the muscles to move very rapidly. This is shivering. As the muscles quickly contract and relax, they produce extra heat to keep the body warm.

DID YOU KNOW

It Makes Sense

Senses do not only detect changes in the surrounding environment. There also are sensory cells inside the body. These cells alert the brain when the body is hungry, thirsty, or tired. They tell the brain when the body hurts and when it needs to get rid of wastes.

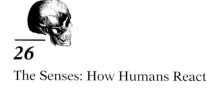

The Senses: How Humans React

On a hot day, or after a person exercises, the body gets too warm. The brain sends messages to get rid of extra heat. The pores in the skin open wide, so that heat can escape. Sweat glands produce sweat, which removes heat from the body.

DID YOU KNOW

No Sweat

As sweat pours out of sweat glands, it spreads over the skin and evaporates. As the sweat evaporates, it takes heat away from the body. Here's a way to demonstrate the cooling effect of evaporation:

Wet one of your fingers. Then rapidly shake the finger back and forth. As the water evaporates, the wet finger will feel much cooler than your other fingers.

A Matter of Degree

Scientists continue to learn new things about the human body almost every day. In 1868, a doctor reported that he had taken more than 1 million readings of people's temperatures. He said that the average temperature of healthy adults was 98.6 degrees F. (37 degrees C.).

For more than 100 years, everyone believed this figure. But in 1992, scientists reported that it was too high. They found that the average temperature of healthy adults is actually 98.2 degrees F. (36.8 degrees C.). They also confirmed that a person's average temperature changes during the day. Body temperature is usually lowest early in the morning and highest in late afternoon.

Twentieth-century doctors think that the higher readings obtained by the 19th-century doctor were due partly to faulty thermometers. The most recent temperature readings were obtained with a number of highly sensitive and very accurate electronic thermometers.

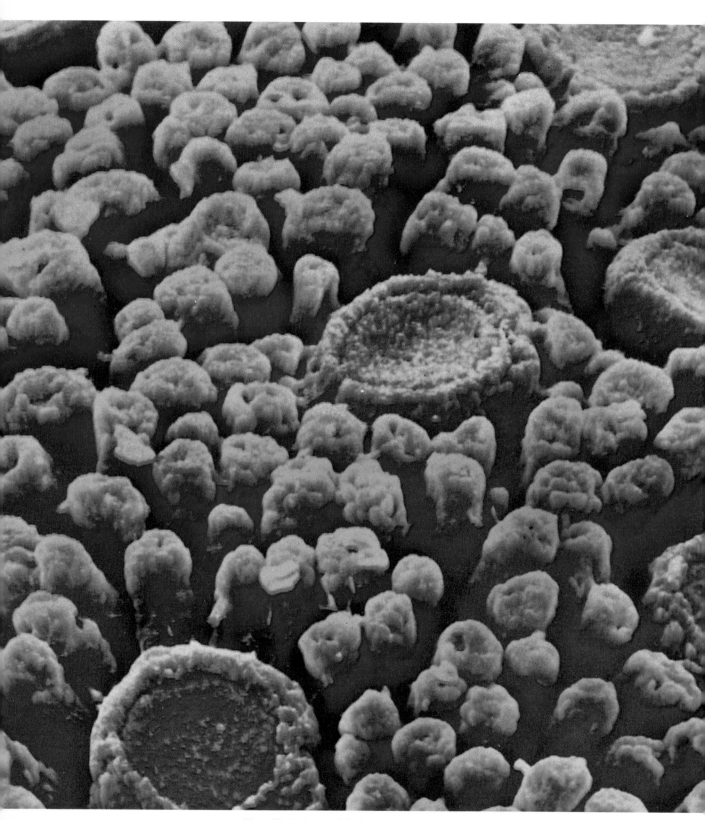

Magnified almost 50 times, the surface of the human tongue reveals its many taste buds (highlighted in purple). With nearly 10,000 taste buds, the average human tongue can detect the four basic taste sensations of bitter, sour, salty, and sweet.

The Sense of Smell

The smell organs of humans, like those of other mammals, are inside the nose. These organs consist of millions of special cells that have hairs called cilia. The cilia constantly move back and forth.

The inside of the nose is kept damp with a sticky liquid called mucus. As a person breathes, air enters the nose. Chemicals in the air mix with the mucus. The moving cilia detect the chemicals and then send messages to nerves, which carry the information to the brain's smell center.

The Sense of Taste

Taste organs are called taste buds. They form little bumps that are spread out over the surface of the tongue. The bumps give the tongue its rough texture. Like the cells that detect smell, taste organs detect chemicals. They can detect four basic tastes: sweet, salt, sour, and bitter. All flavors are made up of a combination of these four tastes.

A human has nearly 10,000 taste buds. Taste buds at the front of the tongue sense mostly sweet and salt. Taste buds at the sides of the tongue detect mostly sour. And the taste buds near the back of the tongue detect mostly bitter.

A human's sense of taste depends heavily on the sense of smell. If you have ever had a cold, you know how true this is! When your nose is stuffed up, you cannot smell food—and it seems as if the food has no taste.

DID YOU KNOW

Smell Well

How many different odors do you think you can recognize? The list is much longer than you might imagine. Scientists have learned that a person with a good sense of smell can distinguish about 10,000 odors!

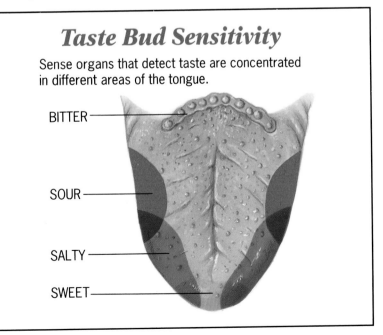

Taste Bud Sensitivity

Sense organs that detect taste are concentrated in different areas of the tongue.

BITTER

SOUR

SALTY

SWEET

Metabolism:
How Humans Function

 Healthy people perform many different tasks during a typical day. They cook meals, wash clothes, take walks, play sports, read books, sing songs, write letters, and do dozens of other things. All of these activities require energy. Even sleeping requires energy!

Like other living things, humans get the energy they need from food. Food also provides materials needed for growth and for regulating the various body processes. Obtaining food and then breaking it down for energy involves many chemical reactions. These reactions, plus the other chemical activities that take place in the body, are called metabolism.

When metabolism works properly, an organism is healthy. It is active and responds to changes in the environment. But when metabolism slows down, the organism does not have enough energy to carry out normal activities. If the processes of metabolism stop, the organism dies.

Opposite:
Like other living things, humans need energy from food in order to function. Obtaining food and breaking it down in the body for energy is part of a process called metabolism.

Eating and Digesting Food

Some animals have very limited diets. A female mosquito feeds only on blood. A herring will eat only microscopic organisms. Horses eat grass.

Humans eat all kinds of things. They eat many different parts of plants and animals. This is a useful adaptation. If certain kinds of foods are not available, humans can eat other foods. They are less likely to starve than animals with limited diets.

Before food can be used by the cells of the body, it has to be broken down into simple chemicals. The process of breaking down food, called digestion, takes place in the digestive system. The main parts of the system are the mouth, esophagus, stomach, and the intestines.

Digestion begins in the mouth as the teeth are used to chew food. A human, like many mammals, has four kinds of teeth. Each kind of tooth is suited to a specific job. Chisel-shaped incisors at the front of the jaw are good for cutting. Pointed canines on either side of the incisors can tear food. Behind the canines are flat-topped premolars and molars, which are best for grinding and crushing food.

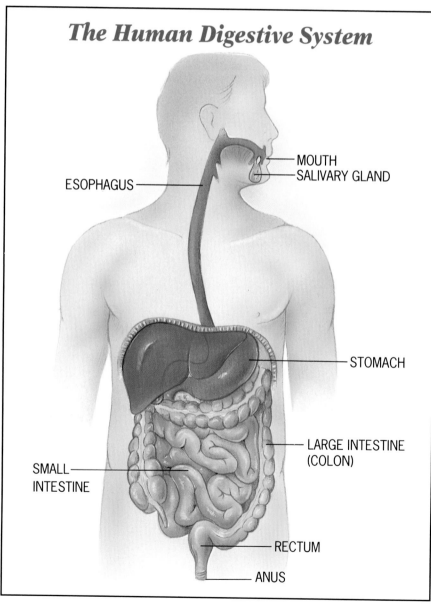

The Human Digestive System

ESOPHAGUS

MOUTH
SALIVARY GLAND

STOMACH

LARGE INTESTINE (COLON)

SMALL INTESTINE

RECTUM

ANUS

Water, Water Everywhere

A very important part of the human diet—and of the human body—is water. About 70 percent of the human body is water. This means if you weigh 100 pounds (45 kilograms), about 70 pounds (32 kilograms) of you is plain water!

Blood is 83 percent water. Muscles are 75 percent water. The brain is 74 percent water. Bone is 22 percent water.

Water is important in many life activities. As the major part of blood, it carries food and other materials throughout the body. It keeps body parts moist so that food and other materials can move in and out of cells. It helps regulate the body's temperature. And it takes part in many chemical reactions, such as enabling cells to release energy from food.

Every day, the human body loses water through respiration, excretion, and perspiration. This water has to be replaced by drinking liquids and eating foods that contain water. Some foods, especially fruits and vegetables, contain large amounts of water. Iceberg lettuce is 96 percent water, watermelon is 93 percent water, and raw carrots are 88 percent water.

Chewing breaks food into smaller pieces, allowing saliva to mix with the food. Saliva moistens and softens food, making it easier to swallow. Saliva also contains a chemical that starts to break down starch, turning it into sugar. You can actually taste this step in digestion by chewing a piece of bread. If you chew the bread enough, it begins to taste sweet.

When a person swallows, food moves from the mouth into the esophagus, which opens into the stomach. The food stays in the stomach for three to four hours, while more digestion takes place. The average human stomach can hold about 3.5 pounds (1.6 kilograms) of food.

The final stages of digestion take place in the small intestine. Then—about 24 hours after the food enters the mouth—the digested particles pass through the wall of the small intestine into the blood. The blood carries the particles to all the cells of the body.

DID YOU KNOW

Something in the Air

Humans need three things to survive: food, water, and air. They can live for many days without food. They may be able to survive for a few days without water. But they can live for only about three minutes without air.

The body contains some extra food and water. But it does not contain extra oxygen. It must constantly take in oxygen, otherwise its cells quickly die.

Metabolism: How Humans Function

Undigested materials must be removed from the body. Muscles push these wastes from the small intestine into the large intestine and to the end of the digestive tube. About once a day, these wastes leave the body through the rectum and out the anus.

Getting Oxygen

To release energy from food, cells need oxygen. All the activities involved in getting and using oxygen make up the process of respiration. The part of respiration that is most familiar to you is breathing.

Humans and other organisms that live on land get the oxygen they need from the air. Air enters and leaves a human body through the nose, and sometimes through the mouth.

As air is breathed in (inspiration), it flows through a tube called the trachea, down into the bronchial tubes, and then into the two lungs. The lungs are

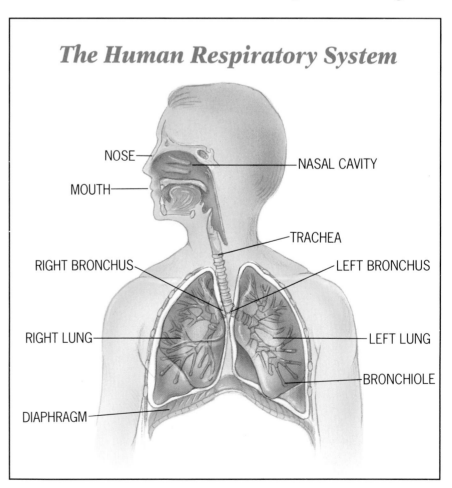

The Human Respiratory System

NOSE

NASAL CAVITY

MOUTH

TRACHEA

RIGHT BRONCHUS

LEFT BRONCHUS

RIGHT LUNG

LEFT LUNG

BRONCHIOLE

DIAPHRAGM

made up of millions of tiny balloon-like structures called alveoli. Each alveolus is surrounded by tiny blood vessels. Oxygen passes from the alveolus into the blood. At the same time, a gas called carbon dioxide moves from the blood into the alveolus. Carbon dioxide is a waste material, produced when the cells break down food for energy. It is removed from the body as the person breathes out (expiration).

Air is moved in and out of the body with the help of certain muscles. One of the most important of these muscles is the diaphragm, which is large and flat and is located between the chest and the abdomen. When a person breathes in, the diaphragm moves down. This makes the chest bigger and causes the lungs to inflate—much like a balloon inflates when you blow air into it. When a person breathes out, the diaphragm moves up. This makes the chest smaller and pushes air out of the lungs. Muscles between the ribs also move to make the chest bigger and smaller.

How the Diaphragm Works

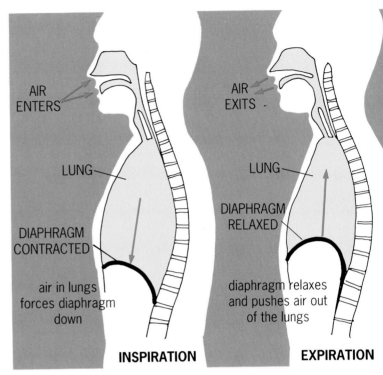

AIR ENTERS

LUNG

DIAPHRAGM CONTRACTED

air in lungs forces diaphragm down

INSPIRATION

AIR EXITS

LUNG

DIAPHRAGM RELAXED

diaphragm relaxes and pushes air out of the lungs

EXPIRATION

Removing Wastes

As the body carries out all of the many functions of life, various wastes are produced that must be removed from the body. The process of removing wastes is called excretion. Undigested foods are excreted through the anus. The waste gas carbon dioxide is filtered through the lungs. Other wastes are filtered through the two kidneys and form a liquid called urine.

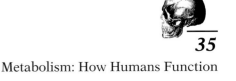

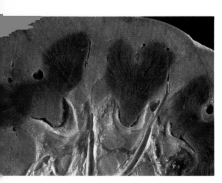
A cross-section of a human kidney.

Human kidneys are dark red structures that are shaped like beans. In fact, kidney beans get their name from their resemblance to kidneys!

Inside each kidney are more than a million tiny filters. When blood flows into a kidney and through the filters, waste materials are removed from it. The wastes, including lots of water, form urine. They collect in a funnel-like space in the kidney and drip down into the urinary bladder. They leave the body when a person urinates.

Circulating Food, Oxygen, and Other Materials

Digestion, respiration, excretion, and all the other processes of metabolism could not take place without the circulatory system. This system acts as the body's transportation network. The circulatory system is made up of the heart, blood vessels, and blood. The heart pumps the blood through the blood vessels, which then carry the blood to all the cells of the body.

Blood vessels are like one-way streets that carry blood in one direction. Vessels called arteries carry blood away from the heart. Other vessels called veins carry blood toward the heart. Connecting the arteries and veins are tiny vessels called capillaries. All movement of materials in and out of the blood takes place through the thin walls of the capillaries.

The human heart The hardest-working muscle in the human body is the heart. When a person sits quietly, the heart contracts—or beats—about 70 times a minute. When a person exercises, the heart beats faster. It may beat as fast as 150 times a minute when a person swims or runs in a race.

The human heart lies in the chest, between the two lungs. Like the hearts of other mammals, the human heart has four rooms, or chambers. The two

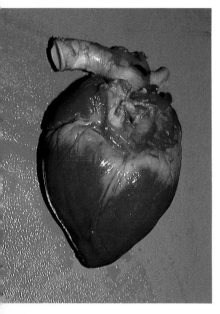
The human heart is a four-chambered muscle that pumps blood throughout the body.

top chambers are called atria. The two bottom chambers are the ventricles. Each atrium opens into the ventricle below it.

Blood that has traveled through the body enters the right atrium. When the muscles in the wall of the right atrium contract, the blood is pushed into the right ventricle. The right ventricle then pumps the blood through the pulmonary artery to the lungs, where carbon dioxide is released and oxygen is picked up. Then the blood flows to the left side of the heart. It enters the left atrium, passes into the left ventricle, and is pumped out through the aorta. The aorta is the largest artery in the body. It branches into smaller arteries that carry the blood to all parts of the body except the lungs.

The heartbeat is controlled by special tissue called the pacemaker, located in the upper part of the right atrium. It makes the heart beat faster when a person is exercising and needs more oxygen. It slows down the heartbeat when a person is resting or sleeping. Sometimes a person's pacemaker stops working correctly. If needed, doctors can put an artificial pacemaker in a person's body to keep the heart beating in its proper rhythm.

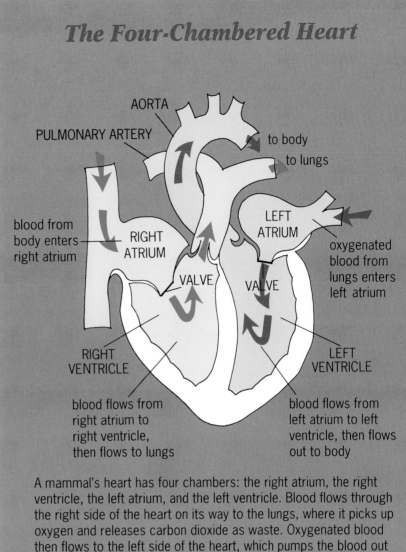

The Four-Chambered Heart

AORTA

PULMONARY ARTERY

to body

to lungs

blood from body enters right atrium

RIGHT ATRIUM

LEFT ATRIUM

oxygenated blood from lungs enters left atrium

VALVE

VALVE

RIGHT VENTRICLE

LEFT VENTRICLE

blood flows from right atrium to right ventricle, then flows to lungs

blood flows from left atrium to left ventricle, then flows out to body

A mammal's heart has four chambers: the right atrium, the right ventricle, the left atrium, and the left ventricle. Blood flows through the right side of the heart on its way to the lungs, where it picks up oxygen and releases carbon dioxide as waste. Oxygenated blood then flows to the left side of the heart, which pumps the blood out to all parts of the body.

DID YOU KNOW

Cell Out

The human body is composed of billions of units called cells. Cells are the building blocks of all living things. Human cells are so tiny that they can be seen only through a microscope.

Imagine that a little drop of your blood covered an area equal to the head of a pin. A drop that size would contain more than 5 million red blood cells.

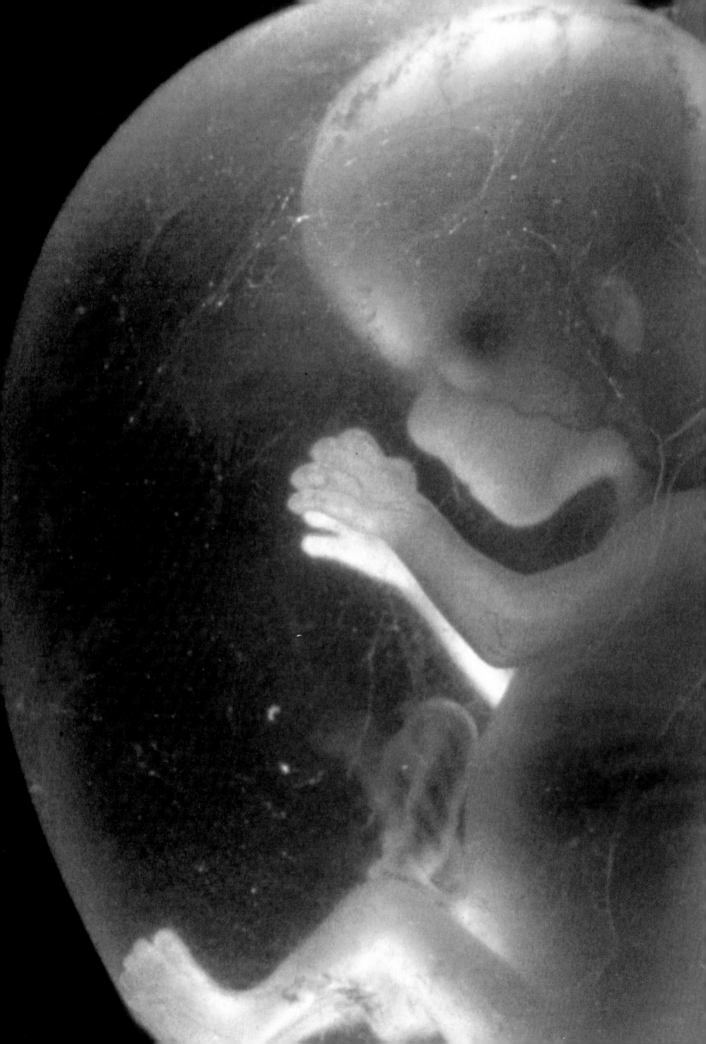

Reproduction and Growth

 One of the most important and most fascinating of the natural processes is the reproduction of living organisms. Reproduction produces new individuals of the same kind. Every kind of organism must reproduce; otherwise the species will die out, or become extinct.

The process of human reproduction is very similar to that of most other mammals. It involves two parents: a mother and a father. A human begins its development within its mother's body. After birth, the baby is fed milk from its mother's mammary glands. It is also cared for until it can provide food and shelter for itself.

But there are differences between human reproduction and reproduction in other mammals. For example, in most mammals reproduction takes place only during a certain time of the year, called the

Opposite:
A human fetus at 14 weeks of age. For a species to survive, its members must reproduce enough offspring to equal those members lost to death.

Compared to other animals, human babies have a very good chance of surviving infancy. Much of this is due to the fact that infants receive a great deal of protection and care from their parents.

mating or breeding season. Humans do not have a special breeding season. They are able to reproduce throughout the year.

Another difference between humans and other mammals is in the amount of care given to the young. Human parents spend many years taking care of their children. As a result, human children have a much better chance than other young mammals of growing up and becoming adults.

The Reproductive System

Reproduction in humans requires two parents, a female and a male. Their reproductive systems produce special cells that must join together to create a new human. The female parent produces cells called eggs; the male parent produces cells called sperm.

The process by which a male's sperm and a female's egg join together is called fertilization.

The female system   The main reproductive organs in a female are the two ovaries and the uterus. Each ovary is about 1 inch (2.5 centimeters) long and shaped like a little almond. Each ovary is connected to the uterus, which is a hollow, muscular organ about the size of a fist.

Eggs are produced in the ovaries. About once a month, an egg leaves one of the ovaries and enters one of the two fallopian tubes. From there, the egg moves slowly toward the uterus. It takes an egg about 24 hours to pass through a fallopian tube. If it is not fertilized by a sperm during this time, it passes through the uterus and out of the body through a short passageway called the vagina, or birth canal.

If the egg is fertilized, it remains in the uterus, where it begins developing into a new human. In approximately 39 weeks, it will be a fully formed baby, ready to be born.

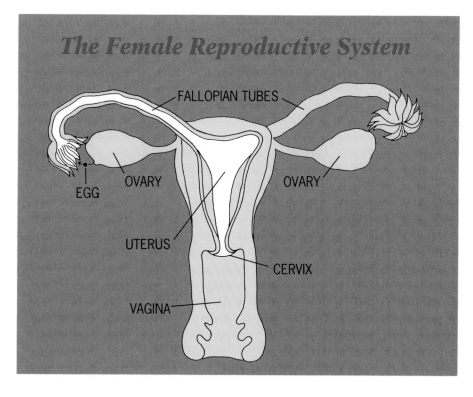

The Female Reproductive System

FALLOPIAN TUBES

EGG

OVARY

OVARY

UTERUS

CERVIX

VAGINA

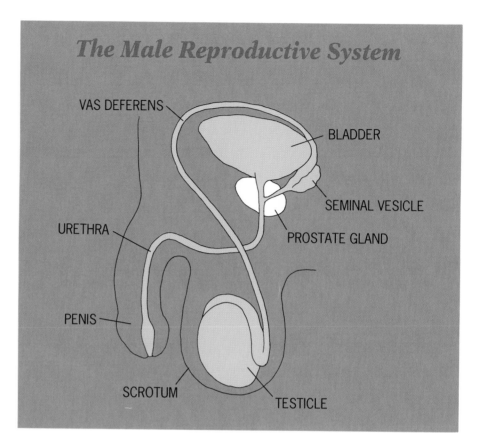

The Male Reproductive System

VAS DEFERENS

BLADDER

SEMINAL VESICLE

URETHRA

PROSTATE GLAND

PENIS

SCROTUM

TESTICLE

A Reproduction Deduction

A human egg is so tiny, it is practically impossible to see without a microscope. But it is huge in comparison with a sperm. An egg is about 2,000 times larger than a sperm. It would take many thousands of sperm to cover the period at the end of this sentence.

An egg is round, like a ball. A sperm looks something like a tadpole. It has a pointed head, a long, threadlike tail, and swims by swinging its tail rapidly back and forth.

The male system The main reproductive organs of a male are the two testes (testicles), which are located in a small pouch of skin called the scrotum. Some cells in the testes produce sperm. Other cells produce a fluid that provides a liquid environment for the sperm. The mixture of sperm and fluid is called semen. Unlike the female system, which produces only one egg each month, the male testes produce millions of sperm at a time. Like eggs, sperm can live for only a short period of time.

Tubes called the vas deferens and the urethra connect the testes to an organ called the penis. During mating, the penis enters the female's vagina and releases as many as 500 million sperm at once. The sperm swim up the vagina, into the uterus, and into the fallopian tubes. If a healthy sperm meets an egg in one of the tubes, fertilization can occur and the woman can become pregnant.

Reproduction and Growth

Development of a Baby

When a sperm enters an egg, the contents of the two cells form one cell. This cell, called the fertilized egg, is the very beginning of a baby. In a matter of days, the fertilized egg divides to form two cells. Then the two cells divide to form four cells. Soon, the four cells divide to form eight cells.

As the cells divide, the egg moves toward the uterus, where it becomes attached to the inner wall. As it divides and grows bigger and bigger, it is called an embryo. Later in its development it will be referred to as a fetus.

A cluster of sperm surrounds an egg (*below left*). Only 4 days after fertilization, a human embryo (*below*) is made up of about 12–16 cells. After 6 days, the cell mass will implant itself in the wall of the uterus.

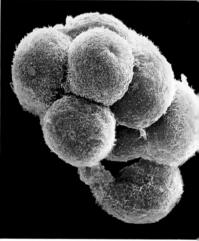

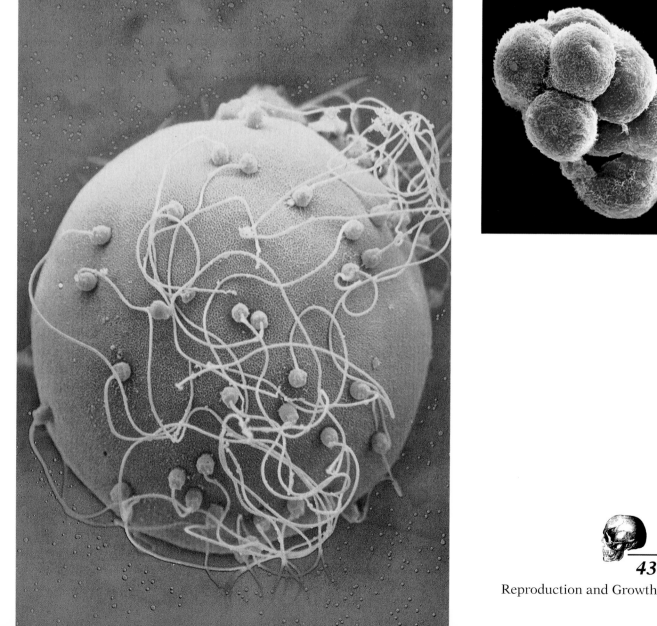

A human embryo at 30 days of age. The mass of tissue on the right will eventually develop into a brain and head.

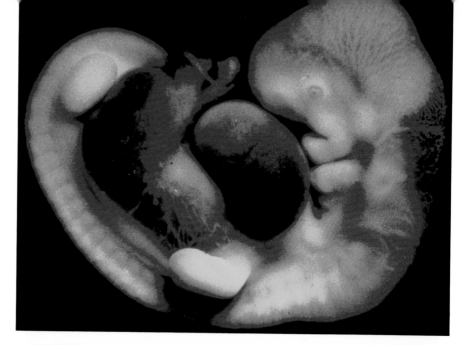

The embryo almost one week later. It is already beginning to form a more recognizable human shape.

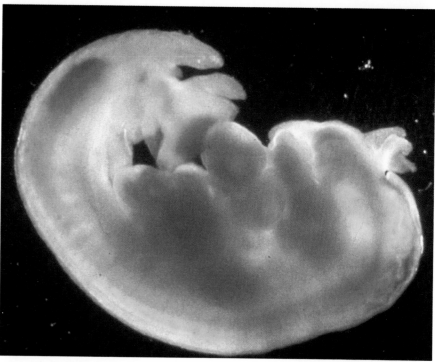

At only 5–6 weeks of age, a head with an eyespot can be seen clearly—along with small buds for hands and feet.

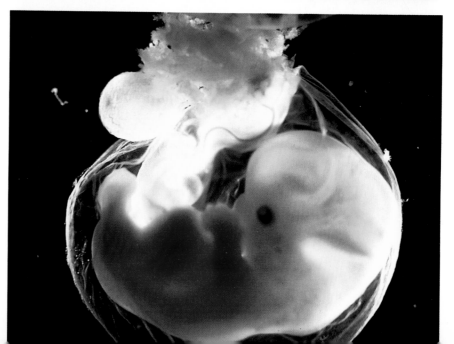

A spongy layer called the placenta connects a developing embryo to the uterus. In the placenta, the blood vessels of the mother and the embryo are very close together. Food and oxygen from the mother's blood pass into the embryo's blood. Carbon dioxide and other wastes produced by the embryo pass into the mother's blood and eventually leave her body.

A human develops within the uterus for about 9 months, or 39 weeks. When a woman isn't pregnant, her uterus is about the size and shape of a fist. During pregnancy, however, the uterus gets very big, as it expands to provide room for the growing baby.

As the cells repeatedly divide, they soon begin to form the various tissues and organs that make up a human body. When an embryo is 4 weeks old, it is about the size of a pencil eraser. At 14 weeks the embryo—now called a fetus—looks very much like a miniature human, although its head is large compared with the rest of its body. At 24 weeks, it is about 12 inches (30 centimeters) long and weighs about 1.5 pounds (0.7 kilogram). It grows rapidly during its last weeks in the uterus. At birth, a normal-size baby weighs about 8 pounds (3.6 kilograms).

During birth, the muscles of the uterus contract. This forces the baby through the birth canal and into the outside world. As soon as the baby has left its mother's body, it begins to move more freely. Its lungs expand and it takes its first breath. Often, this happens as it opens its eyes and its mouth to cry for the first time.

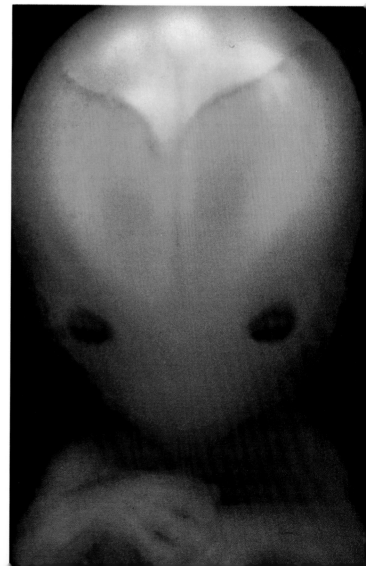

By the end of the third month, most of a fetus's internal organs and external limbs have been developed. At this point, the fetus looks very much like a tiny human.

The Nine Months of Pregnancy

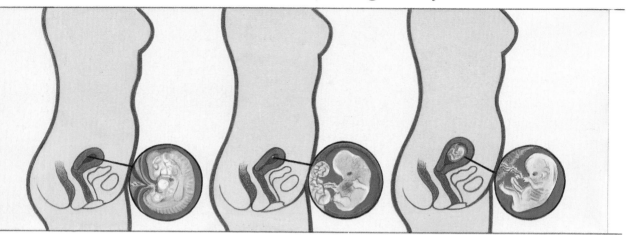

MONTH 1
Embryo has a head and trunk; features begin to form; limb buds appear; heart forms and begins to beat on 25th day. **Length**: about 0.5 inch (1 centimeter). **Weight**: less than 1 ounce (28 grams).

MONTH 2
At the eighth week embryo is called a fetus; has all major body organs and systems, though not completely developed; first bone cells appear; eyelids form but are sealed shut. **Length**: about 1 inch (3 centimeters). **Weight**: less than 1 ounce (28 grams).

MONTH 3
Fingers and toes have soft nails; twenty buds for future teeth; hair begins to appear on head; kidneys develop and secrete urine into bladder; by end of this month fetus is completely formed. **Length**: 4 inches (10 centimeters). **Weight**: just over 1 ounce (28 grams).

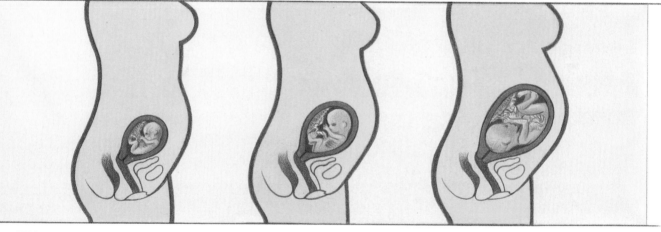

MONTH 4
Now has strong heartbeat, moves, kicks, sleeps and wakes, swallows, and can pass urine. Has eyebrows, small hair on head; skin is pink and transparent. **Length**: 6–7 inches (18 centimeters). **Weight**: about 5 ounces (142 grams).

MONTH 5
Internal organs maturing; sleeps and wakes regularly; much more active; may suck thumb; **Length**: by end of month, 8–12 inches (20–30 centimeters). **Weight**: 0.5–1 pound (227–454 grams).

MONTH 6
Fetus grows rapidly with developing systems; skin is wrinkled and red; body covered with fine hair called lanugo. **Length**: 11–14 inches (about 33 centimeters). **Weight**: about 1–1.5 pounds (about 680 grams).

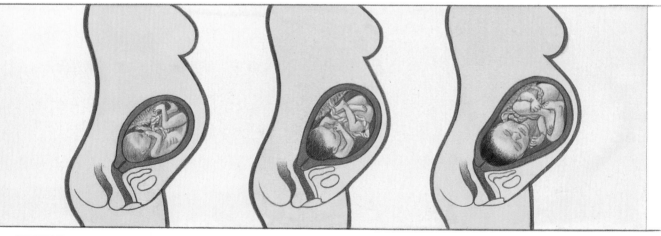

MONTH 7
Exercises by kicking and stretching; sucks thumb; opens and closes eyes; calcium is stored in fetal bone centers. **Length**: about 15 inches (38 centimeters). **Weight**: about 3 pounds (about 1.5 kilograms).

MONTH 8
Too big to move much; bones of head are soft and flexible; **Length**:18 inches (46 centimeters). **Weight**: about 5 pounds (about 2 kilograms).

MONTH 9
Gaining about 0.5 pounds (20 grams) a week; bones in head are soft and flexible for delivery; settles into position head-down against birth canal. At 40 weeks it will be full term and will weigh 6-9 pounds (3–4 kilograms).

From Birth to Adulthood

Some animals are born alone. Their mothers lay eggs that they then abandon. From the moment these animals are born, they must take care of themselves. But no newborn mammals are left alone. Without care from an adult, they would die. Mammal babies depend on adults for food, protection, and shelter.

Like other mammal babies, the first food of most human babies is mother's milk. This milk has all the food substances needed by the baby. It contains sugars, starches, proteins, fats, vitamins, and many minerals. Some of these food substances provide energy. Others are needed to build new cells.

After about nine months of development in the mother's uterus, a human baby is ready to be born. From this moment on, the child will begin to learn how to survive by using the complex processes of language and other forms of communication.

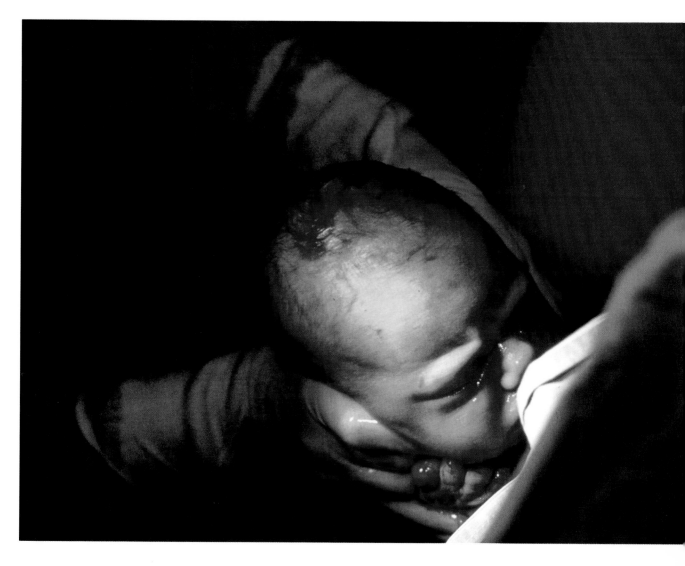

It's a Wonderful Life

Each kind of organism has a certain life span—the length of time from birth until death. Many humans live to be 70 or 80 years old. The highest known age ever reached by a human was 120 years.

Humans have the longest life span of all mammals. But tortoises live longer than humans, and some trees, like the bristlecone pine, live for thousands of years.

The mother's mammary glands in her breasts make milk only after the mother gives birth. The glands continue to make milk until she stops nursing her baby. This usually happens when the baby is about a year old. But even before the baby stops feeding on its mother's milk, it begins to drink other liquids and eat solid foods.

Babies grow quickly during the first year. They learn to do many things. They learn to coordinate their movements, which makes it possible to hold toys and other objects. They learn to pull themselves into a sitting position, and they start to crawl. By the time babies are about a year old, they learn to walk.

Learning never stops. At first, children learn mainly from their parents, and maybe from older brothers and sisters. Then they begin to go to school, where they learn more from teachers. Just like other young mammals, children learn skills that they will need as they grow older.

Sometime between the ages of 10 and 14, children enter a stage called puberty. During this time, their reproductive systems mature. A girl's ovaries begin to release eggs. A boy's testes begin to produce sperm.

Before puberty, girls and boys look very much alike, and their voices are similar. During puberty, many changes take place. For example, girls develop breasts. Boys begin to grow beards, and their voices grow deeper. It becomes very easy to tell girls and boys apart.

Other mammals and many birds also go through big changes as their reproductive systems mature. For example, all baby mallards look alike. But, as a male mallard matures, he grows glossy green feathers on his head and a narrow collar of white feathers around his neck. When he "talks" he says *raeb raeb*. A female mallard grows brownish feathers on her head

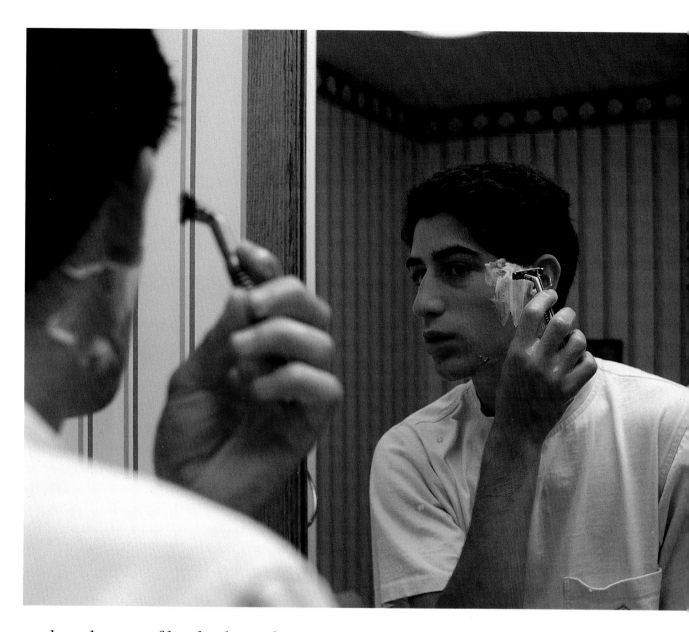

and on the rest of her body as she matures. Her "talk" is a loud *quack quack quack!*

Humans continue to grow until they are in their late teens. By the time they become adults, their bodies have completed their growth in height. But other physical changes take place throughout adulthood. As people grow older, their muscles lose some of their strength. Skin becomes wrinkled and hair turns gray. Changes such as these are part of a natural process called aging. All living things age, traveling along an unavoidable path from birth to death.

Most humans begin puberty between the ages of 10 and 14. During puberty, the human body matures and becomes ready to reproduce. Chemicals in the body called hormones stimulate many changes in the body, including the production of sperm and the growth of facial hair in boys.

Fitting into the Web of Life

To survive, an organism must adapt to its environment. The environment is everything in the organism's surroundings: water, rocks, air—and even other organisms. If an organism cannot successfully fit into its environment, it will die.

Some adaptations are based on how an organism is built. For example, a termite must shed its skin in order to grow. A human has hands that are built to pick up and hold food and other objects.

Other adaptations are based on how an organism's internal systems work. A termite depends on microscopic organisms living in its digestive system to digest the wood it eats. A human eats plant parts such as the fruit of apple trees, but not the wood of apple trees, because a human's digestive system cannot digest wood.

Still other adaptations are based on the things an organism does. When a termite sheds its skin, it also

Opposite:
One way humans have learned to control their environment is by raising their own food. In doing that, humans also create food and nutrients for other living things. Many insects and birds, for example, enjoy feeding on tomatoes as much as humans do.

loses the part of its digestive system that contains the organisms needed to digest wood. To get them back, the termite eats the skin it has shed. Humans have adapted by learning how to farm and raise the plants and animals they use for food.

Competing for Food

Every living thing is part of at least one food chain (a series of relationships based on who eats what). Food chains begin with green plants and algae, which make their own food through a process called photosynthesis. Animals cannot make their own food and so must eat other living things. Some animals eat plants. Other animals eat animals that ate plants.

A very simple food chain is one that starts with grass. Cattle eat grass, and then humans eat cattle. Another food chain begins with microscopic algae in a pond. Microscopic organisms called protozoans eat the algae. Small insects eat the protozoans. Larger insects eat the small insects. A bass eats the large insects. A human catches, and in turn, eats the bass.

Like most animals, humans eat more than one kind of food. Humans are part of many food chains in an environment. They often compete with other animals for food. For example, not all bass are caught and eaten by humans. Some bass are eaten by hawks—and even by other bass.

Humans also compete with other organisms for water, space, soil, and light. Because of humans' greater intelligence, they usually win these competitions. If humans want water for farms and cities, they may lower the levels of lakes and rivers. Animals living in the lakes and rivers cannot stop this. As the water levels fall, competition among the animals for space increases. Many of the animals may die or become easier prey for hawks and other predators.

DID YOU KNOW

Person to Person

Members of the same species do not only compete with other kinds of organisms; they also compete with one another—especially when resources are limited. This is true for all kinds of living things.

As the human population grows, many parts of the world have more people than the environment can support. The people fight to get the food, water, and other things they need. People who are weak and cannot compete for these materials will not be able to survive.

Fitting into the Web of Life

A Typical Food Chain

A. Microscopic algae in a pond.

B. Protozoans eat the algae.

C. Small insects eat the protozoans.

D. Larger animals eat the smaller insects.

E. A bass eats the larger animals.

F. A human eats the bass.

If humans want to catch herring, they use huge fishing nets they have designed and made. With these nets, people catch thousands of herring at a time. A tuna that chases herring, on the other hand, catches one herring at a time. If humans want to build homes, they use bulldozers and other machines to clear away trees on the land. The trees have no defenses to protect themselves against these human actions.

Changing the Environment

The human species has always competed with other species. But as the number of humans has increased, the amount of competition has also increased. Today, many species of plants and animals are in danger of dying out, or becoming extinct, because of harsh competition from humans.

Early humans, who lived more than a million years ago, were not serious competitors to other species. Those humans were few in number. They survived by digging for roots, gathering berries, and using spears and simple traps to catch animals.

Humans are by far the most destructive animals on Earth. As a result of human activities, millions of acres of land have been altered or destroyed, making them useless to other living things.

Population Inflation

Humans learned how to raise plants and domesticate animals about 12,000 years ago. At that time, there were about 15 million people on Earth. With a steady supply of food, fewer people starved relative to the population. The population began to grow rapidly. By the time of Christ, in the year A.D. 1, there were about 250 million people.

It took until the year 1650 for the population to double to 500 million. Since then, each doubling has taken less and less time. By 1850 the population reached 1 billion. Only 80 years later, in 1930, it had doubled to 2 billion. By 1975—just 45 years later—it had doubled again, to about 4 billion.

Some countries have slowed the rate at which their populations increase. People in the United States, Japan, and other places are having fewer children. But the world's population continues to grow rapidly. By 1993, there were 5.5 billion people on Earth. By the end of the 1990s, the total is expected to be about 6.4 billion.

How will the growing human population affect you and your family? How will it affect the lives of your children? How will it affect other living things? In many ways, it will mean increased competition among all humans for the Earth's precious resources.

Gradually, humans used their superior intelligence to take more and more control of their environment. Soon, they discovered how to control fire. Then they discovered how to farm plants and domesticate animals. They learned to mine coal and to make tools from metals. They built towns and roads, dams and factories, automobiles and airports.

As the population has grown, humans have made many changes in the environment. Grasslands filled with wildflowers have been turned into fields of corn. Marshes and other wetlands have been drained to build shopping centers. Forests have been cut down and replaced by houses. Changes like these have affected the populations of many species of plants and animals.

Overhunting has also hurt the populations of many species. Scientists believe that in the early 1800s, there were about 225,000 blue whales on

Pollution caused by humans and their activities has caused widespread damage to the environment. Toxic waste dumping and use of pesticides have harmed many plant and animal populations, bringing many species close to extinction.

Earth. Then people began to use modern ships and weapons to hunt blue whales. They killed the whales faster than the animals were able to reproduce. Today, there are fewer than 2,000 blue whales left. Hunting blue whales is now against the law, but it may still be too late to save the species from extinction.

Chemical poisons—called pesticides—produced by humans have also harmed many organisms. They are used to kill pests, such as insects that eat crops or cause disease. But chemical pesticides do not only kill pests. They also kill helpful organisms. Many birds and fish, for example, have been killed by chemical pesticides.

Whenever pesticides and other harmful chemicals are dumped into the environment, the environment becomes polluted. This harms the habitats of many organisms, and hurts humans, too. For example, humans often dump oil, chemicals from factories, and untreated garbage into lakes and rivers. These wastes kill food fish and also make the water unfit for drinking and swimming.

The Last Passenger

Once upon a time, passenger pigeons were very common in North America. They were attractive birds, with bluish-gray feathers covering their backs and white feathers on their bellies. They lived in huge groups called flocks. Some of these flocks contained more than 1 billion birds! In spring and fall, when the passenger pigeons migrated, the sky became dark. There were so many birds that they blocked out the sun.

Passenger pigeons lived and built their nests in oak and maple forests that covered large areas of North America. During the 1800s, people chopped down many of the forests. This destroyed the pigeons' homes and nesting places. People also hunted the pigeons, killing them by the millions. They killed the pigeons faster than new pigeons were born and raised.

Soon, huge flocks of passenger pigeons no longer darkened the sky. The population of passenger pigeons became smaller and smaller. Finally, only one passenger pigeon remained. She lived in the zoo in Cincinnati, Ohio, and was named Martha, in honor of George Washington's wife.

Martha died on September 1, 1914. With her death, passenger pigeons became extinct. No one will ever again see a living member of this species.

Recycle, Reuse, Cure the Wasteful Blues

Each year, millions of trees are cut down and turned into paper. Every time a tree is cut down, homes for birds and other animals are destroyed.

You can help protect the homes and lives of forest creatures by wasting less paper. Saving paper is one of the easiest and most helpful things you can do to improve and preserve the environment.

There are many other simple things you can do to help conserve wood resources. Instead of using new paper for notes, use scrap paper, such as the back side of old school papers. For drinking, use a glass instead of a paper cup. Reuse paper bags from the grocery store when you go shopping and don't purchase products that come with lots of extra plastic and cardboard packaging.

Recycling is important, too. Recycle newspapers and other wastepaper so that they can be turned into new papers. A ton of paper made from wastepaper saves 17 trees!

Recycling other products is another effective and important way to help the environment. Reusing glass, aluminum, and cardboard greatly reduces the amount of waste that needs to be dumped in landfill garbage sites.

Recycling helps to protect the environment.

Saving the Environment

Humans are the ruling organisms on Earth and the most powerful of all living things. We have the power to destroy other organisms, but we also have the power to protect and save them, too.

Many people know it is very important to protect the environment. They work hard to solve the problems of pollution and to protect wild plants and animals. Everyone—including you!—can be part of this effort. There are many things that each person can do to help make sure that other species survive.

Taking care of the environment and all the creatures that live on Earth helps humans, too. It helps make the Earth a healthier, safer place in which to live. And it helps make sure that humans and all other living things will continue to survive on this beautiful planet for many centuries to come.

THE ANIMAL KINGDOM

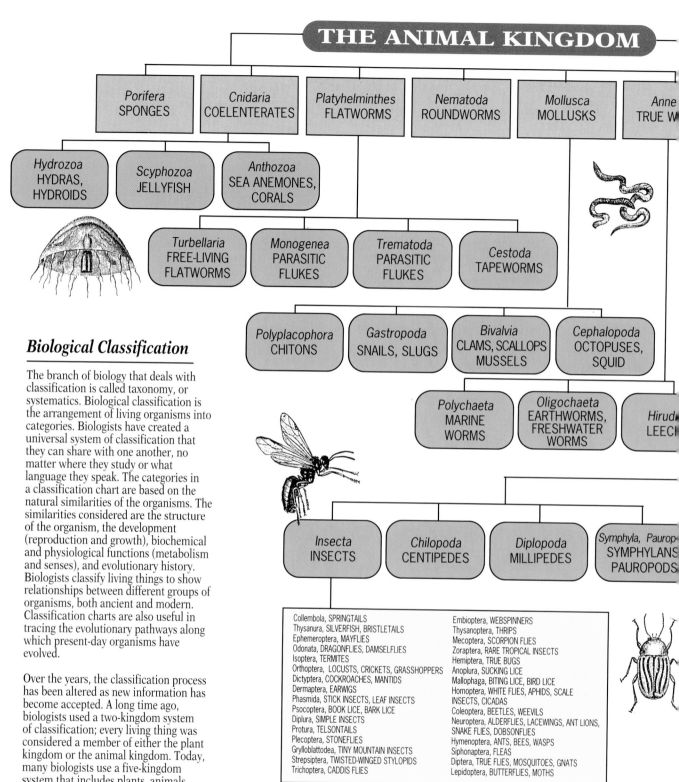

Porifera SPONGES

Cnidaria COELENTERATES

Platyhelminthes FLATWORMS

Nematoda ROUNDWORMS

Mollusca MOLLUSKS

Anne TRUE W

Hydrozoa HYDRAS, HYDROIDS

Scyphozoa JELLYFISH

Anthozoa SEA ANEMONES, CORALS

Turbellaria FREE-LIVING FLATWORMS

Monogenea PARASITIC FLUKES

Trematoda PARASITIC FLUKES

Cestoda TAPEWORMS

Polyplacophora CHITONS

Gastropoda SNAILS, SLUGS

Bivalvia CLAMS, SCALLOPS MUSSELS

Cephalopoda OCTOPUSES, SQUID

Polychaeta MARINE WORMS

Oligochaeta EARTHWORMS, FRESHWATER WORMS

Hirud LEEC

Insecta INSECTS

Chilopoda CENTIPEDES

Diplopoda MILLIPEDES

Symphyla, Paurop SYMPHYLANS PAUROPODS

Biological Classification

The branch of biology that deals with classification is called taxonomy, or systematics. Biological classification is the arrangement of living organisms into categories. Biologists have created a universal system of classification that they can share with one another, no matter where they study or what language they speak. The categories in a classification chart are based on the natural similarities of the organisms. The similarities considered are the structure of the organism, the development (reproduction and growth), biochemical and physiological functions (metabolism and senses), and evolutionary history. Biologists classify living things to show relationships between different groups of organisms, both ancient and modern. Classification charts are also useful in tracing the evolutionary pathways along which present-day organisms have evolved.

Over the years, the classification process has been altered as new information has become accepted. A long time ago, biologists used a two-kingdom system of classification; every living thing was considered a member of either the plant kingdom or the animal kingdom. Today, many biologists use a five-kingdom system that includes plants, animals, monera (microbes), protista (protozoa and certain molds), and fungi (non-green plants). In every kingdom, however, the hierarchy of classification remains the same. In this chart, groupings go from the most general categories (at the top) down to groups that are more and more specific. The most general grouping is PHYLUM. The most specific is ORDER. To use the chart, you may want to find the familiar name of an organism in a CLASS or ORDER box and then trace its classification upward until you reach its PHYLUM.

Collembola, SPRINGTAILS
Thysanura, SILVERFISH, BRISTLETAILS
Ephemeroptera, MAYFLIES
Odonata, DRAGONFLIES, DAMSELFLIES
Isoptera, TERMITES
Orthoptera, LOCUSTS, CRICKETS, GRASSHOPPERS
Dictyptera, COCKROACHES, MANTIDS
Dermaptera, EARWIGS
Phasmida, STICK INSECTS, LEAF INSECTS
Psocoptera, BOOK LICE, BARK LICE
Diplura, SIMPLE INSECTS
Protura, TELSONTAILS
Plecoptera, STONEFLIES
Grylloblattodea, TINY MOUNTAIN INSECTS
Strepsiptera, TWISTED-WINGED STYLOPIDS
Trichoptera, CADDIS FLIES

Embioptera, WEBSPINNERS
Thysanoptera, THRIPS
Mecoptera, SCORPION FLIES
Zoraptera, RARE TROPICAL INSECTS
Hemiptera, TRUE BUGS
Anoplura, SUCKING LICE
Mallophaga, BITING LICE, BIRD LICE
Homoptera, WHITE FLIES, APHIDS, SCALE INSECTS, CICADAS
Coleoptera, BEETLES, WEEVILS
Neuroptera, ALDERFLIES, LACEWINGS, ANT LIONS, SNAKE FLIES, DOBSONFLIES
Hymenoptera, ANTS, BEES, WASPS
Siphonaptera, FLEAS
Diptera, TRUE FLIES, MOSQUITOES, GNATS
Lepidoptera, BUTTERFLIES, MOTHS

Insectivora, INSECTIVORES (e.g., shrews, moles, hedgehogs)
Chiroptera, BATS
Dermoptera, FLYING LEMURS
Edentata, ANTEATERS, SLOTHS, ARMADILLOS
Pholidota, PANGOLINS
Primates, PROSIMIANS (e.g., lemurs, tarsiers, monkeys, apes, humans)
Rodentia, RODENTS (e.g., squirrels, rats, beavers, mice, porcupines)
Lagomorpha, RABBITS, HARES, PIKAS
Cetacea, WHALES, DOLPHINS, PORPOISES

Carnivora, CARNIVORES (e.g., cats, dogs, weasels, bears, hy
Pinnipedia, SEALS, SEA LIONS, WALRUSES
Tubulidentata, AARDVARKS
Hyracoidea, HYRAXES
Proboscidea, ELEPHANTS
Sirenia, SEA COWS (e.g., manatees, dugongs)
Perissodactyla, ODD-TOED HOOFED MAMMALS (e.g., horses, rhinoceroses, tapirs)
Artiodactyla, EVEN-TOED HOOFED MAMMALS (e.g., hogs, ca camels, hippopotamuses)

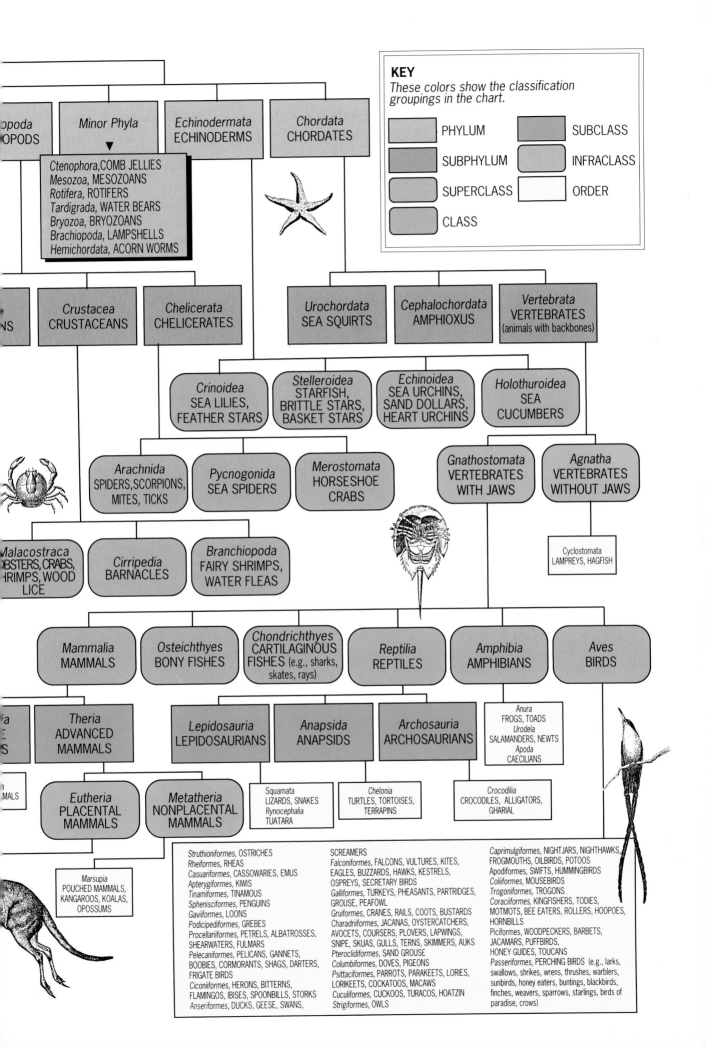

KEY
These colors show the classification groupings in the chart.

- PHYLUM
- SUBPHYLUM
- SUPERCLASS
- CLASS
- SUBCLASS
- INFRACLASS
- ORDER

...opoda
...OPODS

Minor Phyla ▼

Ctenophora, COMB JELLIES
Mesozoa, MESOZOANS
Rotifera, ROTIFERS
Tardigrada, WATER BEARS
Bryozoa, BRYOZOANS
Brachiopoda, LAMPSHELLS
Hemichordata, ACORN WORMS

Echinodermata ECHINODERMS

Chordata CHORDATES

...NS

Crustacea CRUSTACEANS

Chelicerata CHELICERATES

Urochordata SEA SQUIRTS

Cephalochordata AMPHIOXUS

Vertebrata VERTEBRATES (animals with backbones)

Crinoidea SEA LILIES, FEATHER STARS

Stelleroidea STARFISH, BRITTLE STARS, BASKET STARS

Echinoidea SEA URCHINS, SAND DOLLARS, HEART URCHINS

Holothuroidea SEA CUCUMBERS

Arachnida SPIDERS, SCORPIONS, MITES, TICKS

Pycnogonida SEA SPIDERS

Merostomata HORSESHOE CRABS

Gnathostomata VERTEBRATES WITH JAWS

Agnatha VERTEBRATES WITHOUT JAWS

Malacostraca ...OBSTERS, CRABS, ...HRIMPS, WOOD LICE

Cirripedia BARNACLES

Branchiopoda FAIRY SHRIMPS, WATER FLEAS

Cyclostomata LAMPREYS, HAGFISH

Mammalia MAMMALS

Osteichthyes BONY FISHES

Chondrichthyes CARTILAGINOUS FISHES (e.g., sharks, skates, rays)

Reptilia REPTILES

Amphibia AMPHIBIANS

Aves BIRDS

...ia ...E ...S

Theria ADVANCED MAMMALS

Lepidosauria LEPIDOSAURIANS

Anapsida ANAPSIDS

Archosauria ARCHOSAURIANS

Anura FROGS, TOADS
Urodela SALAMANDERS, NEWTS
Apoda CAECILIANS

...MALS

Eutheria PLACENTAL MAMMALS

Metatheria NONPLACENTAL MAMMALS

Squamata LIZARDS, SNAKES
Rynocephalia TUATARA

Chelonia TURTLES, TORTOISES, TERRAPINS

Crocodilia CROCODILES, ALLIGATORS, GHARIAL

Marsupia POUCHED MAMMALS, KANGAROOS, KOALAS, OPOSSUMS

Struthioniformes, OSTRICHES
Rheiformes, RHEAS
Casuariiformes, CASSOWARIES, EMUS
Apterygiformes, KIWIS
Tinamiformes, TINAMOUS
Sphenisciformes, PENGUINS
Gaviiformes, LOONS
Podicipediformes, GREBES
Procellariiformes, PETRELS, ALBATROSSES, SHEARWATERS, FULMARS
Pelecaniformes, PELICANS, GANNETS, BOOBIES, CORMORANTS, SHAGS, DARTERS, FRIGATE BIRDS
Ciconiiformes, HERONS, BITTERNS, FLAMINGOS, IBISES, SPOONBILLS, STORKS
Anseriformes, DUCKS, GEESE, SWANS,

SCREAMERS
Falconiformes, FALCONS, VULTURES, KITES, EAGLES, BUZZARDS, HAWKS, KESTRELS, OSPREYS, SECRETARY BIRDS
Galliformes, TURKEYS, PHEASANTS, PARTRIDGES, GROUSE, PEAFOWL
Gruiformes, CRANES, RAILS, COOTS, BUSTARDS
Charadriiformes, JACANAS, OYSTERCATCHERS, AVOCETS, COURSERS, PLOVERS, LAPWINGS, SNIPE, SKUAS, GULLS, TERNS, SKIMMERS, AUKS
Pteroclidiformes, SAND GROUSE
Columbiformes, DOVES, PIGEONS
Psittaciformes, PARROTS, PARAKEETS, LORIES, LORIKEETS, COCKATOOS, MACAWS
Cuculiformes, CUCKOOS, TURACOS, HOATZIN
Strigiformes, OWLS

Caprimulgiformes, NIGHTJARS, NIGHTHAWKS, FROGMOUTHS, OILBIRDS, POTOOS
Apodiformes, SWIFTS, HUMMINGBIRDS
Coliiformes, MOUSEBIRDS
Trogoniformes, TROGONS
Coraciiformes, KINGFISHERS, TODIES, MOTMOTS, BEE EATERS, ROLLERS, HOOPOES, HORNBILLS
Piciformes, WOODPECKERS, BARBETS, JACAMARS, PUFFBIRDS, HONEY GUIDES, TOUCANS
Passeriformes, PERCHING BIRDS (e.g., larks, swallows, shrikes, wrens, thrushes, warblers, sunbirds, honey eaters, buntings, blackbirds, finches, weavers, sparrows, starlings, birds of paradise, crows)

Glossary

adaptation A body part or behavior that helps an organism survive in its environment.

alveolus One of millions of tiny air sacs in the lungs through which oxygen enters the body.

anus The opening at the end of the large intestine through which undigested wastes are excreted.

aorta The largest artery in the body.

arteries Blood vessels that carry blood away from the heart.

atrium A chamber in the heart that receives blood from veins.

binocular vision The use of both eyes to see in three dimensions.

capillaries Tiny blood vessels through which blood flows from the arteries to the veins.

cells The building blocks of all living things.

cerebrum The part of a human's brain that is the center for intelligence, memory, and judgment.

cones Light-sensitive cells in the eye that are most sensitive in bright light and that register color.

diaphragm A muscle between the chest and the abdomen that helps in breathing.

digestion The mechanical and chemical breakdown of food into substances the body can use for growth and energy.

domesticate To tame.

eardrum A thin membrane that separates the outer ear from the middle ear.

egg The female reproductive cell, which is fertilized by a sperm from the male parent.

embryo An organism in the early stages of its development.

endothermic Warm-blooded, with a body temperature that stays more or less the same.

environment The surroundings of an organism or group of organisms.

esophagus The structure through which food passes from the mouth to the stomach.

evolution Change over a long period of time.

excretion The removal of wastes from the body.

extinct No longer in existence.

fertilization The union of sperm and egg, which leads to the development of a new organism.

fingerprint A pattern of ridges on the tip of a finger.

food chain The order in which organisms feed on one another.

fossils Remains or traces of organisms that lived in the past.

lens A clear structure near the front of the eye through which light passes to the retina.

mammary gland A milk-producing organ in female mammals.

metabolism The chemical processes in cells that are essential to life.

ovaries Female organs that produce eggs.

penis The male organ used during mating to release sperm into the female's reproductive system.

placenta The structure that connects the embryo to the uterus.

predator An animal that kills other animals for food.

primates The group of mammals that includes apes, monkeys, lemurs, and humans.

puberty The time at the end of childhood when reproductive systems mature.

reproduction The process by which organisms create other members of their species.

respiration The process by which organisms take in oxygen and use it to release energy from foods.

retina A light-sensitive coating on the back of the eye, like the film of a camera.

rods Light-sensitive cells in the retina of the eye that are most sensitive in dim light and that register only black and white.

saliva A liquid secreted into the mouth that moistens food and begins the process of digestion.

scrotum A sac-like pouch that contains the testes.

semen A fluid produced by the male reproductive system that contains sperm.

semicircular canals Structures in the inner ear that help to maintain a sense of balance.

species A group of organisms that share many traits with one another and that can reproduce with one another.

sperm The male reproductive cell that fertilizes a female egg.

testes Male organs that produce sperm.

urine Liquid wastes produced in the kidneys.

uterus The female organ in which the embryo develops.

vagina The birth canal through which a baby is born.

veins Blood vessels that carry blood toward the heart.

ventricle A chamber in the heart that pumps blood out into arteries.

vertebrae The bones that make up the backbone.

vertebrate An animal with a backbone.

For Further Reading

Ardley, Neil. *Science Book of the Senses.* San Diego, CA: Harcourt Brace Jovanovich Juvenile Books, 1992.

Asimov, Isaac. *How Did We Find Out about Our Human Roots?* New York: Walker & Co., 1979.

Bell, Neill. *Only Human: Why We Are the Way We Are.* New York: Little, Brown & Co., 1983.

Blashfield, Jean F. and Black, Wallace B. *Recycling.* Chicago: Childrens Press, 1991.

Coville, Bruce. *Prehistoric People.* New York: Doubleday, 1990.

Markham, Adam. *The Environment.* Vero Beach, FL: Rourke Corp., 1988.

Martin, Paul D. *Messengers to the Brain: Your Fantastic Five Senses.* Washington, D.C.: National Geographic Society, 1984.

Micallef, Mary. *Listening: The Basic Connection.* Carthage, IL: Good Apple, 1984.

Newman, Matt and Lemay, Nita K. *Human Reproductive Systems.* Chicago: Society for Visual Education, 1980.

Parker, Steve. *The Brain & Nervous System.* New York: Franklin Watts, 1991.

Parker, Steve. *Nerves to Senses: Projects with Biology.* New York: Franklin Watts, 1991.

Parker, Steve. *Touch, Taste & Smell.* New York: Franklin Watts, 1991.

Stein, Sara B. *Making Babies.* New York: Walker & Co., 1984.

Twist, Clint. *Reproduction to Birth: Projects with Biology.* New York: Franklin Watts, 1991.

Zim, Herbert S. *Your Stomach & Digestive Tract.* New York: Morrow Junior Books, 1973.

_____. *Food & Digestion.* Morristown, NJ: Silver Burdett Press, 1988.

_____. *Heart & Blood.* Morristown, NJ: Silver Burdett Press, 1988.

_____. *Lungs & Breathing.* Morristown, NJ: Silver Burdett Press, 1988.

Index

Algae, 52
Alveoli, 35
Aorta, 37
Ape, 9
Artery, 36
Atria, 37
Australopithecine, 17 (photo)

Backbone, 8, 11
Balance (sense of), 24–25
Binocular vision, 21
Birth, 47 (photo)
Birth canal, 41, 45
Brain, 9, 10–12, 10 (artwork), 20
Breast-feeding, 8 (photo)
Bronchial tubes, 34

Capillary, 36
Carbon dioxide, 35, 37, 45
Cell, 37
Cerebellum, 10
Cerebral cortex, 12
Cerebrum, 11–12
Cilia, 29
Circulation, 36–37
Coclea, 23
Color-blindness, 20
Cones, 20, 21
Cortex, 11

Decibel, 22
Dermis, 25
Diaphragm, 35 (diagram)
Diet, 32
Digestion, 32–34, 36
Digestive system, 32 (artwork), 51

Ear, 22–23, 24
    anatomy, 23 (artwork)
    inner, 22, 23, 25
    middle, 22, 23
    outer, 22
Eardrum, 22–23
Early humans, 14–15 (artwork), 15–17,
    16–17 (photos)
Egg, 40, 42, 43 (photo), 48
Embryo, 43 (photo), 44 (photo), 45
Endothermic, 9
Environment, 7, 51, 54–57
Epidermis, 25
Esophagus, 32, 33
Evolution, 17
Excretion, 33, 35–36
Expiration, 35
Extinction, 17, 39, 54, 56
Eye, 20–21, 20 (photo), 25
    anatomy, 21 (artwork)

Fallopian tube, 41
Fertilization, 41, 42–43
Fetus, 43, 45 (photo)
Fingerprint, 11
Food chain, 52–54
Fossil, 17

Growth, 47–49

Hair, 9
Hand, 14–15
Heart, 36–37, 36 (photo), 37 (diagram)
Homo habilis, 14, 15 (artwork)
Homo sapien, 13
Hypodermis, 25
Hypothalamus, 11

Incus, 23
Inspiration, 34
Intelligence, 12
Intestine, 32, 33–34

Kidney, 35–36, 36 (photo)

Language, 12–13
Lemur, 9
Lens, 20

Malleus, 23
Mamma, 8
Mammal, 8–9, 20, 24, 29, 39, 47
Mammary glands, 8, 39, 48
Mating, 39–40
Medulla, 10, 11
Metabolism, 31–37
Monkey, 9
Mouth, 32, 33
Mucus, 29

Neanderthals, 15 (artwork), 16

Optic nerve, 21
Ovaries, 41
Oxygen, 33, 34–35, 37, 45

Pacemaker, 37
Passenger pigeon, 56
Penis, 42
Perspiration, 33
Pesticides, 56
Photosynthesis, 52
Placenta, 45
Pollution, 56, 57
Posture, 13–14, 13 (artwork)
Pregnancy, 42, 46 (diagram)
Primate, 9
Protozoan, 52
Puberty, 48

Recycling, 57 (photo)
Reproduction, 39–46
Reproductive system, 40–42

female, 41 (diagram)
male, 42 (diagram)
Respiration, 33, 34–35, 36
Respiratory system, 34 (artwork)
Retina, 21
Rod, 21

Scrotum, 42
Semen, 42
Semicircular canals, 24–25
Sense organs, 11, 19–20, 22
Senses, 19–29
    See also Balance, Ear, Eye, Skin,
    Smell, Taste, Temperature.
Skin, 25
    anatomy, 26 (artwork)
    sense cells, 25
Soundwave, 22
Sperm, 40, 42, 43 (photo)
Spinal cord, 11
Stapes, 23
Stomach, 32, 33

Taste (sense of), 20, 29
Taste bud, 28 (photo), 29 (artwork)
Teeth (kinds of), 32
Temperature (sense of), 26–27
Testes, 42, 48
    See also Testicles.
Testicles, 42
Three-dimensional image, 20, 21
Tongue, 28 (photo), 29 (artwork)
Toxic waste, 56
Trachea, 34

Urethra, 42
Urine, 35, 36
Uterus, 41, 42, 45

Vagina, 41, 42
    See also Birth canal.
Vas deferens, 42
Vein, 36
Ventricle, 37
Vertebrae. *See* Backbone.
Vertebrate, 8